The North American INDIANS

The Marshall Cavendish illustrated history of

The North American INDIANS

A Way of Life

MARSHALL CAVENDISH
New York • London • Toronto • Sydney

Library Edition Published 1991

© Marshall Cavendish Limited 1991
© Pemberton Press Limited 1991

Published by Marshall Cavendish Corporation
2415 Jerusalem Avenue
Bellmore
N.Y. 11710

Series created by Graham Beehag Books
Produced by Pemberton Press Limited

Designed by Graham Beehag
Illustrated by Kerry Bridge
Edited by Maggi McCormick

All rights reserved. No part of this book may be reproduced or utilized
in any form or by any means electronic or mechanical including photocopying,
recording, or by any information storage and retrieval system, without
permission from the copyright holders.

Library of Congress Cataloging-in Publication Data

Oakley, Ruth,
  The Marshall Cavendish illustrated history of the North American
Indians / Ruth Ena Oakley. – Limited ed.
      p. cm.
   Contents: v.1, In the beginning – v.2, Homes, food and clothing – v.3,
A way of life – v.4, Religion and customs – v.5, Art and totems
– v.6, Conflict of cultures.
       ISBN 1-85435-137-0 (set)
   1. Indians of North America – Juvenile literature. [1. Indians of
North America.] I. Marshall Cavendish Corporation. II. Title.
E77.4.O18   1990
970.004'97–dc20   89-17371
                                                                 CIP
                                                                 AC

Printed and bound in the United States by Lake Book Manufacturing Inc.

Contents

Then and now	6
Clans and families	6
Phratries, Moities and tribes	8
Sachems and tribal government	9
The league of the Iroquois	11
Shamans and societies	12
Rules of behavior	15
Love, marriage, and divorce	15
Men, women, and children	17
Education	18
Games	23
War	25
Coups	27
Captives	31
Weapons	32
Hunting	38
Animals the Indians hunted	34
Ways of hunting	41
Fishing	45
Farming	49
Trade	54
Travel and transport	55
Glossary	57
Table of tribes	59
Maps of tribal areas	61
Map of major linguistic areas	62
Index	63
Index of tribes	64

Then and now
One of the main differences between the everyday life of the North American Indian and our own time was the lack of machinery available to the Indians. The Indians did not develop the use of the wheel to save work and effort; it was introduced to them by the European settlers. We only have to remember how much inconvenience a power failure causes us to realize how much we take electricity, gas, and steam power for granted. Ever since the Industrial Revolution in Europe in the eighteenth and nineteenth centuries, western civilization has been firmly based on the development of technology and on trade.

We should not assume, however, that because native Americans did not have automobiles or air-conditioning that they could not live in comfort and contentment. Much depended on where they lived and their position in their own society. We should remember, for instance, that the civilizations of ancient Egypt, Greece, and Rome made great contributions to the history of the world with very few machines and "modern" conveniences.

Clans and families
Most tribes were organized into fairly small groups,

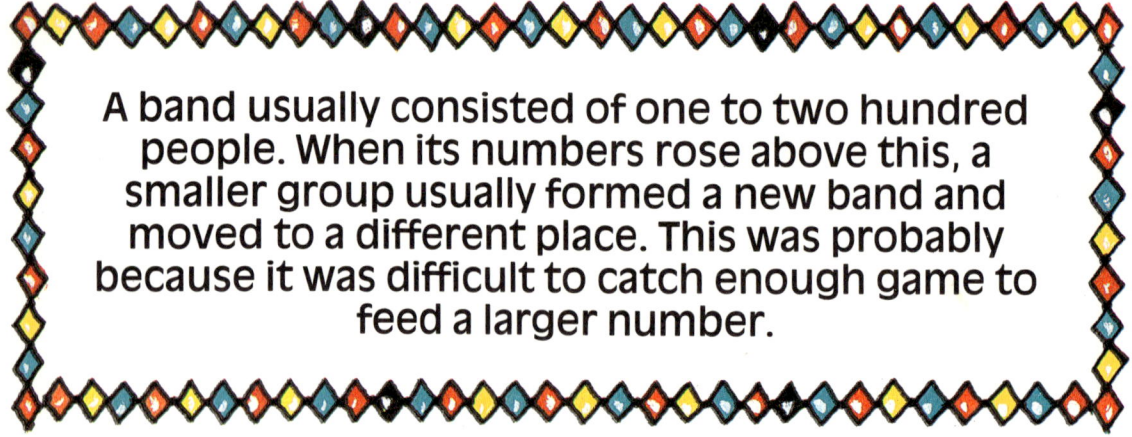

A band usually consisted of one to two hundred people. When its numbers rose above this, a smaller group usually formed a new band and moved to a different place. This was probably because it was difficult to catch enough game to feed a larger number.

The famous painter of Indians, George Catlin, portrayed these Comanches in their tepee village in 1834. The women are preparing buffalo hides for tanning.

called clans, in which each individual was known and respected and had a definite part to play. The clan was made up of a group of related families. All the members of a clan were related by blood, and each member had to marry someone from outside the clan.

The tribal notion of a family was broader than our own. Relatives such as aunts and uncles had a closer relationship with mother, father, and children than is the case in most modern American families, and they were allowed to exercise more authority over children. Grandmothers were particularly important and influential.

Each clan had its own totem, or guardian spirit, which gave the clan its name. For example, the Eagle clan would have been guided and protected by the spirit of the eagle, and all eagles would have been sacred to that clan. They would have respected eagles and would not have hunted or eaten them; the spirit of the eagle would have been regarded as their ancestor and would have been the focus of their religious ceremonies.

Phratries, moieties, and tribes

A phratry was a group of clans. Phratries combined to form moieties; a moiety was half of a tribe. Most tribes were divided this way. The Haida were divided into "Ravens" and "Eagles." The Pueblo peoples are still organized into moieties today: one moiety rules for half of the year, and the other group takes over for the remaining six months of each year.

Generally, Indian society was very democratic. Birth did not usually determine a person's class or caste. Everyone began life with equal rights and opportunities. Members of the tribe gained respect, power, or privileges through their own efforts and abilities including healing skills, ability to fight well, and wisdom.

The only exception to this general principle was the social organization of the Natchez, which was based on a rigid class system determined by birth. Even among the Natchez, however, there was movement between the classes by marriage.

The Nookta Indians of the northwest coast used to hunt whales. They sailed in special canoes which held six men and used huge harpoons. When Captain James Cook made contact with them in 1776, he counted 95 canoes. From this, he estimated their population to be about 2,000. There were 3,135 Nookta living in British Columbia in 1967.

Sachems and tribal government
The two main groups of people who achieved special positions were the chiefs, or sachems, and the shamans. A chief was a man greatly respected and admired by the rest of the tribe. However, few chiefs

The rivers and waterways were the main trade and travel routes for the Indians, and they devised several methods of boat building. There were boats made from tree trunks, birch bark, planks, reeds, and skins. The Ojibwa used a canoe which was fifteen feet long. Because it was made of birch bark, it was light enought to be carried between rapids or from one river to another. The women sewed the pieces of bark together with the roots of pine trees, and the joints and gaps were made watertight by coating them with pine resin.

had absolute power, like a King or Queen, and the title was not inherited.

Chiefs were generally chosen or elected by the tribe and were dignified and wise. They gave advice which the tribe usually followed, and they led the tribe in times of war. Some tribes had two chiefs: one advised on daily peacetime matters; another acted as a war leader. Camps and bands also had local chiefs, who helped the tribal chief and advised on specific concerns. A council of elders, men of age and experience, also helped the chief to administer justice and decide punishments for offenses.

The punishment for murder was death, either of the murderer or of one of the male members of his family if he had escaped. Other offenses such as stealing, swearing, and assaulting or insulting another member of the tribe were punished by being flogged, fined, or scratched with sharp thorns.

Left: Two of the four Iroquois chiefs who visited England in 1710 to persuade the British government to defend its frontiers in North America against colonists who were encroaching on Indian tribal lands.

The League of the Iroquois

The League of the Iroquois was a confederation of six tribes which had a Council of fifty chiefs. They met several times a year to discuss and decide matters which affected all the clans of the Mohawk, the

---

The Carrier tribe lived in the interior of British Columbia near Bear Lake. Their name is believed to derive from their habit of making widows carry on their backs the charred bones of their deceased husbands. When the men went to war, they wore "armor" made either from strips of wood or from the hide of a moose which had been coated with fine pebbles.

11

Oneida, the Cayuga, the Onondaga, the Seneca, and the Tuscarora tribes. The clans had the right to elect a sachem to the Council, and the old women who were the heads of the clans organized the elections.

Right: Medicine men.

Shamans and societies

The medicine man, or shaman, was also a person of great importance and prestige. It was difficult to become a shaman; a person had to prove that he had special healing and magic powers.

Societies and clubs were an important feature of tribal social life. There were many kinds, for men and women, young and old. Some were secret and others entirely open. There were societies for dancing, war, healing, and religion. Sometimes, a society covered several tribes, such as the Grand Medicine Society of the Ojibwa, the Omaha, and the Winnebago.

Left: Europeans had romantic ideas of how Indians courted each other.

Below: An eighteenth-century French painter imagined that this is how the Canadian Indians celebrated a marriage.

Rules of behavior

Native Americans lived close together in small communities. Because they often needed to cooperate to survive in difficult circumstances, there were strict conventions and rules of behavior, which applied to such things as courtship, marriage, children's upbringing, and the care of the elderly.

Love, marriage, and divorce

Customs varied from tribe to tribe, but marriages were generally arranged, rather than left to young people to decide completely for themselves. Marriage took place at an earlier age than we are used to. A couple who really disliked each other would not be forced to marry, however. Also, a young man might court a girl he wanted as his wife and persuade her and her parents to agree to their marriage.

In "Black Elk Speaks" by John G. Neihardt, Black Elk, a medicine man of the Oglala Sioux, tells the

story of High Horse and his endeavors to win the girl he loved. Among the Plains Indians, there were strict rules about meetings between young men and women. High Horse had to go to a great deal of trouble even to speak to the girl to try to make her like him.

Eventually, he joined a raid on a Crow village and stole some horses. This proved to the girl's parents that he was a man worthy of her, so they allowed him to marry her.

In most tribes, one man had one wife, and one woman one husband, although among some prairie tribes, one man might have several wives, who were often sisters. Divorce was possible and was usually signaled by a simple announcement on either side. Nevertheless, divorce was not undertaken lightly; and among the prairie tribes, divorce was considered shameful. Among the Navajo, a woman who wished to divorce her husband simply put his saddle and belongings outside the door, and he had to leave.

Men, women, and children

Men and women each had their roles to play. In some tribes, men were dominant; in others, it was the women. In some tribes, the children took their descent from their mothers, and in others from their fathers. Sometimes, as with the Navajo, the women owned the property such as the family's home and belongings. Among the Iroquois, women, not men, of the tribe had the power to choose the clan chiefs (who were men).

Generally, the men went hunting and fishing, and the women stayed at home and prepared and cooked the food. The women and children left the village to gather fruits and nuts, and to fish. Among the

Women and children tended the crops.

Iroquois, the men cleared the forest for planting, and the women tended the fields. The men made most of the household tools. On the Pacific coast, men built the wooden houses and canoes. The women generally did the sewing and made pottery. In some tribes, the men did the weaving. On the Plains, the women set up the tepees.

Mothers and grandmothers were generally the dominant influences over young children. Fathers and uncles took over the boys as they grew up, when they were taught to hunt and were initiated into the men's societies.

Education

Although Indian children did not go to school, they had a lot to learn from an early age. They had to learn the practical skills on which they would depend as adults. Girls learned to cook, weave, look after babies, farm, and forage. Boys learned to use weapons, hunt, fish, and forage. These lessons began when a child was only three or four years old.

Children were frequently tattooed at that age, and boys particularly had to endure ordeals, such as plunging into an icy river in winter. These tests were done not to be cruel, but to make the children tough and brave so that they could survive as adults.

Right: Children had many skills to learn.

The Haida used a large cedar log to make a canoe seventy feet long. It could carry three tons of cargo and needed sixty men to paddle it. To make a warship, two of these canoes were joined together by roping a deck made of planks between them.

Children were also taught the history and morals of their tribe. In the evenings, the old men of the tribe re-told the ancient stories and folk tales that made up the tribe's traditions.

Left: A Nez Perce mother with her baby in a decorated cradleboard.

Right: A moss bag.

Babies

Babies and toddlers were treated kindly and fussed over. Many tribes used cradleboards to carry babies. Algonquin babies of the Eastern Woodlands were carried around in "moss bags" made of leather which were laced down the front. On the back of the bag was a loop so the bag could be hung up or carried around.

Some tribes tied the bag to a board. It usually had a shelf at the bottom for the baby's feet to rest on, and a hoop of wood at the top protected the baby's head if the board fell over. Charms were sometimes hung from the hoop to amuse the infant and protect her from evil spirits. The bag was lined with moss to protect the baby and keep her warm.

Left: An Apache woman with a baby on a wooden cradleboard which has a hood of reeds decorated with beads and shells.

In some tribes, the cradleboards were beautifully decorated and passed down the generations as family heirlooms. In other tribes, such as the Salish of British Columbia, however, no cradle could be used for more than one baby. The Kutenai decorated their cradles with beads, as did the prairie tribes. The Kutchin of the Northwest Territories made cradles of birch bark. The Flatheads of the Northwest Plateau got their name from their custom of pressing a flap on the cradleboard against their babies' foreheads, which caused them to become distorted and slope back.

Games

Life was not all work, and the Indians, both men and women, enjoyed periods of relaxation when they played games and had athletic contests of wrestling,

Below: Life was not all work.

running, archery, bowling hoops with sticks, and throwing spears along the ground in the snow. Lacrosse, football, and shinny were also played. In British Columbia, the ball was made of fungus sewn up in elk skin. Cat's Cradle and juggling were enjoyed indoors in the winter evenings, as was gambling with dice, sticks, or straws.

Indian women gambling outside a tepee.

War

Warfare was not a matter of large armies facing each other and fighting according to drills and regulations. Before the Indians learned the battle techniques of the white man, a small group of young braves, under the leadership of a war chief, usually made a surprise attack to steal the horses or kill the

Blackfeet and their tepees in Glacier National Park, Montana, photographed in 1915.

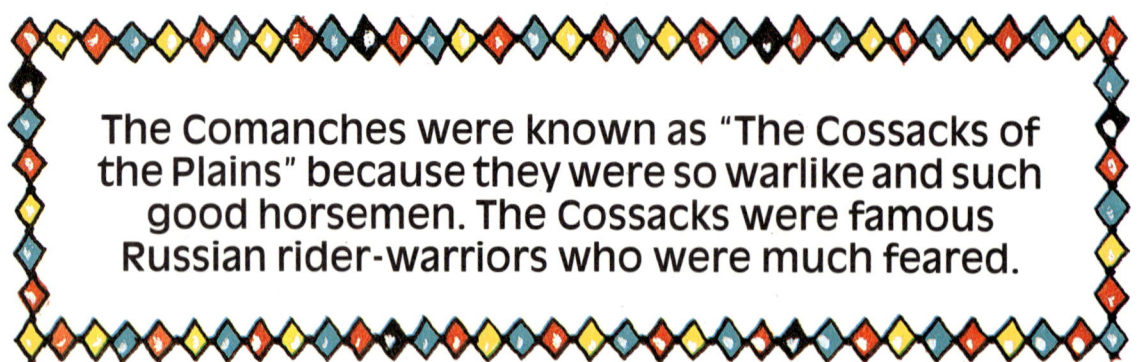

The Comanches were known as "The Cossacks of the Plains" because they were so warlike and such good horsemen. The Cossacks were famous Russian rider-warriors who were much feared.

inhabitants of a nearby enemy village.

These raids often took place under the cover of darkness. Once the villagers under attack had gathered themselves to retaliate, it was not considered shameful for the raiding party to make their escape. Similarly, if a warrior had a dream or a vision advising him not to set out, or not to continue once he had set out, no one thought less of him for heeding the warning and returning home.

Preparations were carefully organized, but once the attack was launched, it was every man for himself, with no one in charge supervising maneuvers.

The reasons for the attacks varied. Sometimes, there were disagreements over territory. Other times, it was just a desire to plunder goods or steal horses. A successful raiding party provided a young brave with a way to achieve prestige, which might help him to win power or arrange a good marriage.

Right: An Indian warrior's bravery could be measured from the number of feathers on his coup stick.

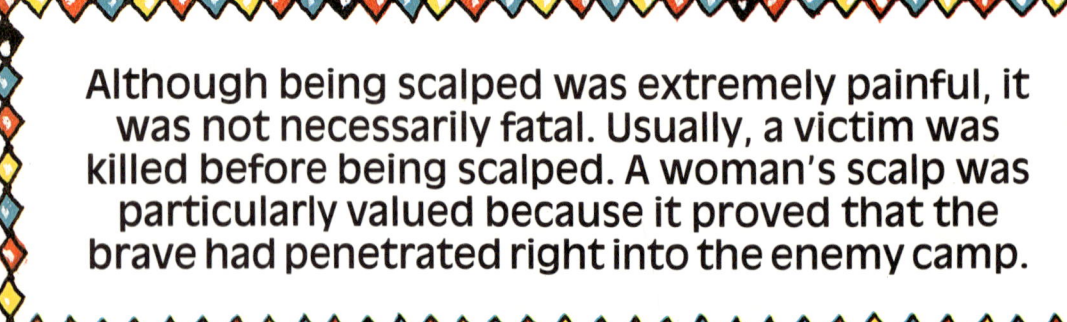

Although being scalped was extremely painful, it was not necessarily fatal. Usually, a victim was killed before being scalped. A woman's scalp was particularly valued because it proved that the brave had penetrated right into the enemy camp.

Coup

Among the tribes of the Plains, there was a system of grading a brave's achievements, which was called "counting coup." Young warriors carried wands made of willow and decorated with feathers, which were known as "coup sticks." The highest scoring honor was achieved by touching an enemy with this stick or with the hand. Killing or scalping an enemy and stealing a horse were other ways of counting coup. Other people could tell a man's war record by the feathers he wore in his hair and the marks he painted on his face.

Most Indians fought on foot and by stealth, launching surprise attacks if possible. The Plains Indians fought on horseback after the arrival of the European settlers. This made a surprise attack difficult, because it was hard to keep the horses quiet.

A battle with the Indians on horseback involved fierce hand-to-hand fighting.

For most tribes, these skirmishes were irregular interludes: most of the time, they were busy hunting and providing food and shelter for their families. Some tribes, however, such as the Apache and the Comanche, were very warlike and aggressive.

Left: This portrait of Kishkekosh, a Fox brave, painted in 1837 shows him wearing a buffalo skull and war paint and carrying a coup stick. Each feather on the stick denotes a brave deed.

Captives

The Apache and the Comanche were particularly cruel to captives and tortured them for as long as possible before they finally died. Many tribes carried out the custom of scalping, cutting the skin around the head and peeling off a layer of skin with the hair attached. Captured scalps were dried and used as decoration for the warrior.

Despite such activities, most tribes treated their captives kindly once the heat of the battle was over. There are accounts of Europeans who did not wish to return to their own people after experiencing tribal life, but many captives were simply used as slaves by the victorious tribe.

Right: Some tribes tortured their captives.

The scalping of enemies was common among the Algonkian tribes of the Eastern Woodlands. Sometimes, the whole head and the hands were cut off as well. The eating of an enemy's heart was believed to pass on his courage to the brave who ate it.

Weapons

Before the arrival of the first Spanish explorers, the Indians were still Stone Age people. Their weapons and armor were all made of wood, stone, or bone. The most usual weapons were bows and arrows, clubs, knives, harpoons, and spears.

Until the introduction of the horse, most tribes used long bows. The Prairie tribes found them

unwieldy to use on horseback, so they changed to shorter ones. Bows were usually made of ash or willow. The shafts of the arrows were made of willow or saskatoon, and the heads were originally fashioned from bone, antler, or stone. The Interior Salish of British Columbia were unusual among North American Indians in using poisoned arrows. The poison was obtained either from the venom of

The Indians were skillful fighters with a wide variety of weapons.

rattlesnakes or the roots of poisonous plants.

Stone clubs with sharp teeth or stones set in them were effective weapons in the close hand-to-hand fighting which the Indians practiced. Some warriors, especially among the Eastern Woodland tribes, were also able to throw these clubs with deadly accuracy.

Stone-bladed knives set in a handle of wood or bone, which were normally used for hunting and day-to-day requirements, were also used in warfare. As the Indians began to trade with the early trappers and settlers, they acquired steel knives, hatchets, and axes, or tomahawks, which they used in war as well as for peaceful purposes. Thus, many white men and women were killed with weapons manufactured by their compatriots.

Armor As a defense against their original weapons, the Indians devised several forms of protective clothing or armor. Among the peoples of the Eastern Woodlands and of British Columbia, armor was generally made of slats of wood laced together to make a tunic which would protect the chest and back against a spear or arrow. The Slave tribe of Northwest Canada used woven willow twigs.

Shields The other universal form of protection was the shield. The Iroquois made theirs from a wicker framework covered with tough rawhide. The

Right: Short Bull, a Sioux, wears an armor tunic made of wood.

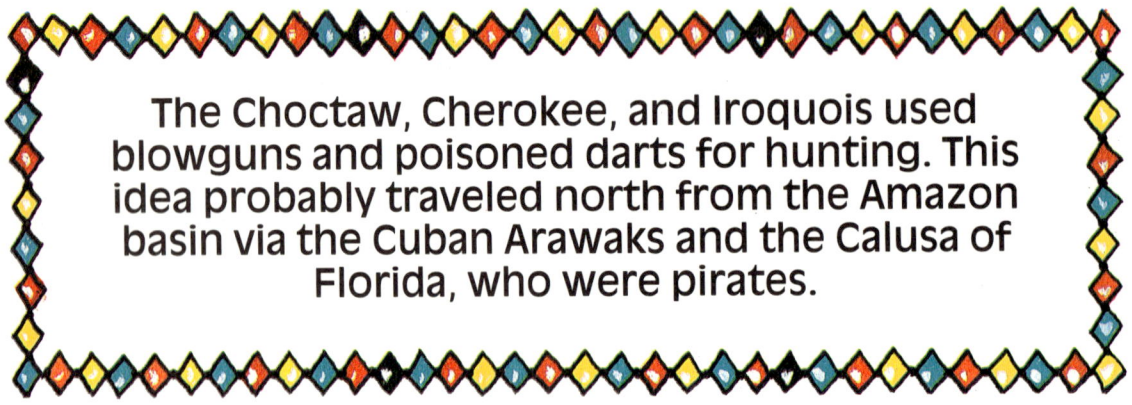

The Choctaw, Cherokee, and Iroquois used blowguns and poisoned darts for hunting. This idea probably traveled north from the Amazon basin via the Cuban Arawaks and the Calusa of Florida, who were pirates.

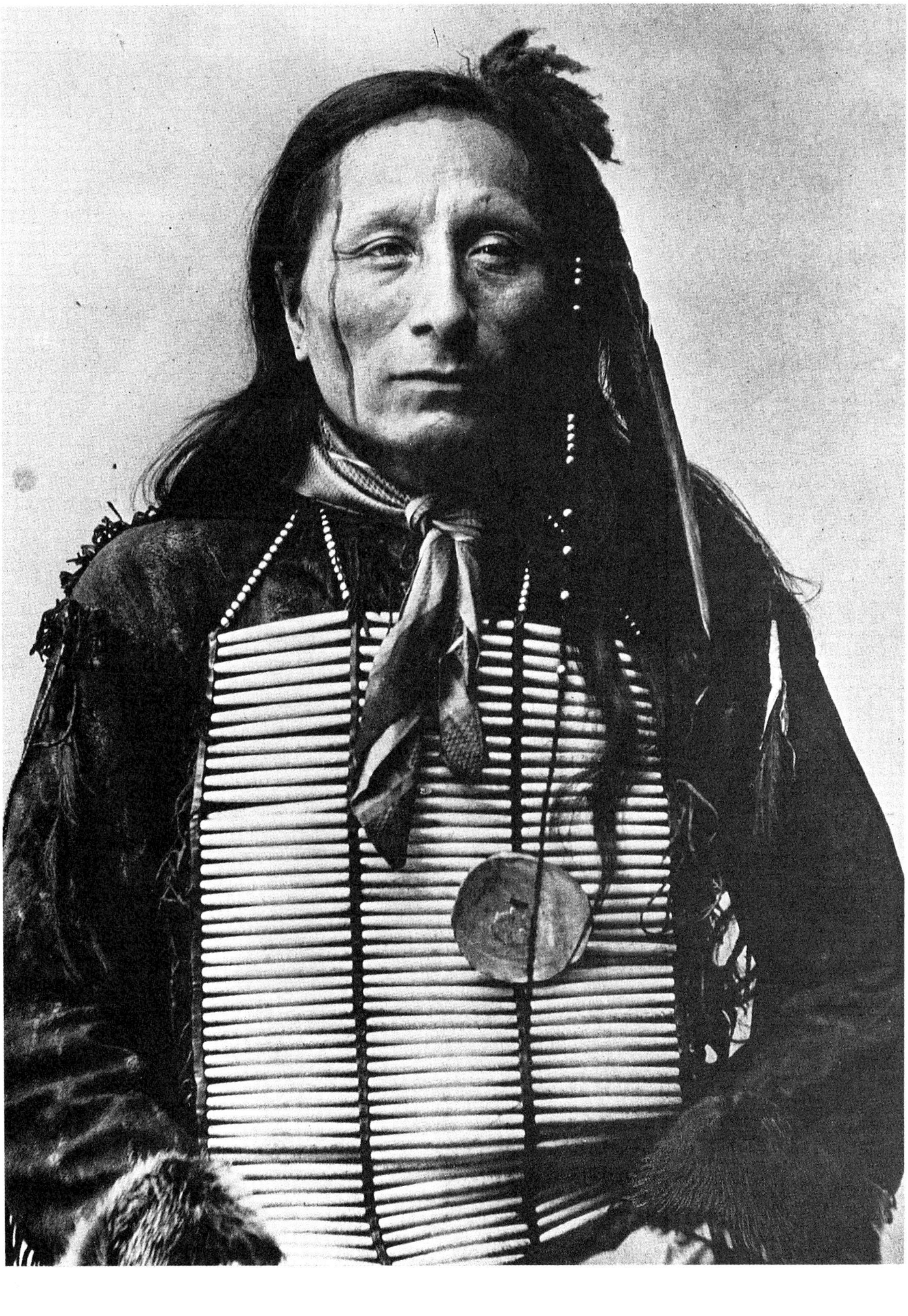

36

Left: Two types of Indian shield.

Below: Apache scouts helped the Americans track down Geronimo.

Indians of the Plains used round shields made of the heavy skin taken from the chest of an old bull buffalo.

The shields were often beautifully painted, hung with charms, and decorated with feathers. The designs were often revealed in dreams, and shields were believed by the Plains Indians to have magic powers. When they were not in use, shields were kept carefully wrapped up so that the magic did not leak out.

Guns A shield made from several layers of tough hide will provide excellent protection against a spear or an arrow, but the Indians had no defense against bullets. The tribes who traded for muzzle-loading guns gained immediate, deadly superiority over neighboring tribes. For example, a small group of Micmac wiped out the Beothuk of Newfoundland in the early 1700s, because the Micmacs had guns and the Beothuks only had bows and arrows.

Hunting

The skills and weapons which the Indian used in warfare were used more regularly—and more constructively—in hunting animals for food and clothing. Indians did not kill animals for sport until after the introduction of the horse by the Spanish, when some of the Plains tribes killed more buffalo than they needed. Nor did they look on animals as an inferior form of life. To the Indian, animals were a source of reverence and admiration because he recognized the superiority of the animals' senses. He knew that most animals have better sight, keener hearing, a more developed sense of smell, and greater speed than humans.

No tribe would kill the bird or animal that was sacred to the clan. In addition, a hunter apologized to the spirit of any animal he had killed and was careful to observe the correct rituals before, during, and after hunting. All tribes were particularly in awe of the large grizzly bears found in the Rocky Mountains, which could easily kill a man.

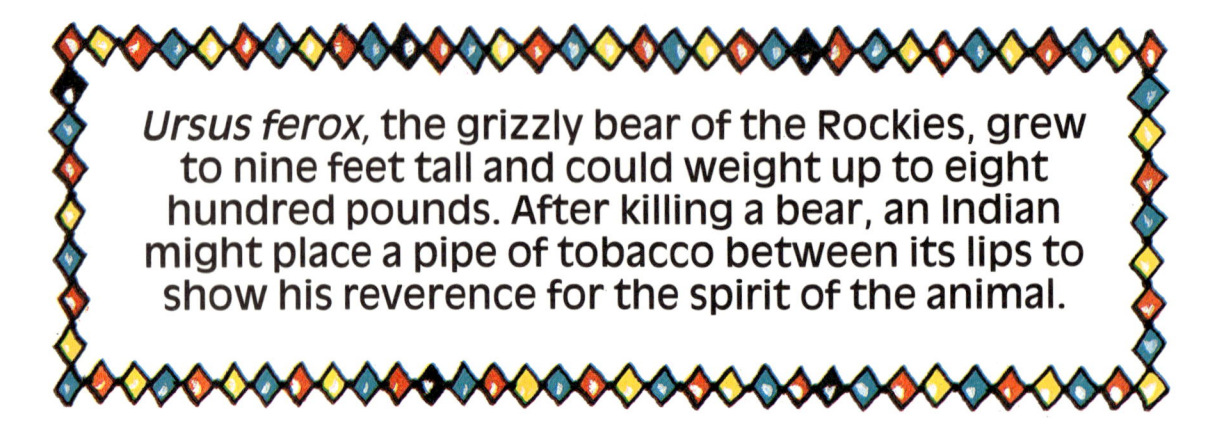

Ursus ferox, the grizzly bear of the Rockies, grew to nine feet tall and could weight up to eight hundred pounds. After killing a bear, an Indian might place a pipe of tobacco between its lips to show his reverence for the spirit of the animal.

Because of their dependence on the natural world for their livelihood, Indians were very observant and knowledgeable about the habits of the creatures which they hunted. Most of their hunting was done on foot with bows and arrows, and they used their knowledge and intelligence to overcome the superior strength and speed of their prey.

Animals the Indian hunted

Among the large game which they hunted were moose, elk, caribou, and reindeer in the snows of the north and the buffalo of the Plains. Also four species of bear provided furs and meat: the polar bear of the north, the grizzly, the black, and the brown.

Small game included the common or Virginia mule, and blacktailed deer; pronghorn antelope;

Indian hunters disguised with the heads and skins of deer were able to approach their prey near enough to shoot them with bow and arrow.

A bolas is a weapon made by tying heavy stones to a strong cord. The Indians of Louisiana used bolases to bring down ducks and other game birds. The Pomo people used clay pellets and a sling.

bighorn, or argali sheep, of the Rockies; gray, white, pied, dusty, and black wolves; coyote; fox and Arctic fox. Other small mammals which were prized included the wolverine, raccoon, rabbit, ermine, mink, badger, squirrel, beaver, porcupine and any other small mammals local to an area.

Ways of hunting

Sometimes, a brave went off alone to hunt, or a small group formed a hunting party: at other times, a large group of men and boys joined a communal hunt. The tribes of the Great Basin made large nets which they spread across the mouth of a canyon. Then, with the help of their dogs, they drove large numbers of jackrabbits into the traps. Similarly, buffalo were sometimes driven over the edge of a ravine or lured into territory favorable to the hunters.

Hunting in wolf skins.

The Indians knew many hunting techniques. They were adept at constructing pits and snares. They wore the skins and heads of the animal they were stalking to enable them to approach the animals to within range of their arrows. They imitated

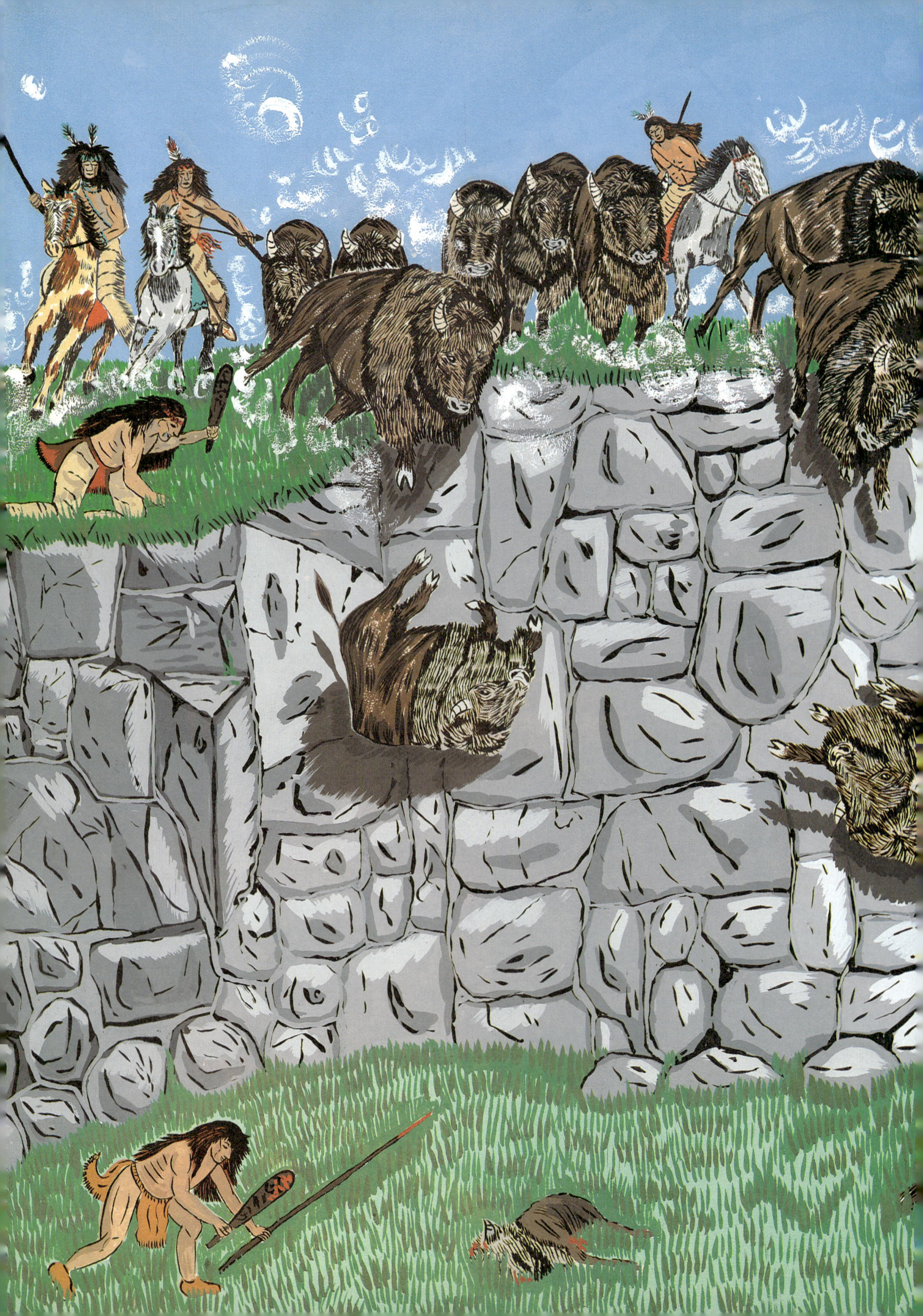

Stampeding buffalo over the edge of a cliff was one of the Indians' hunting methods.

the calls of the animals they hunted to decoy them into approaching the waiting, hidden hunters.

In his books, Chief Kah-ge-ga-gah-bowh of the Ojibwa related four different ways in which the people of his tribe killed deer before the introduction of guns.

One was to make a snare of wild hemp, which was placed where it could catch the deer around the neck. The more the deer struggled, the tighter it pulled the noose until it was strangled.

Another involved observing the path that the deer normally took. The hunters drove sharp spikes of wood into the ground and hid them behind a log.

Hunting rabbits and foxes.

The unsuspecting herd leapt over the log onto the spikes, which would pierce and kill some of them.

If the deer were driven into water or across snow, out of their natural element, they soon became tired and thus became easy targets for the hunters' spears and knives.

Before attempting to shoot deer with a bow and arrow, the Ojibwa looked for tracks and observed carefully from the woods as the deer came to their "Salt Licks" at the water's edge. The tribe generally hunted at night, either by using a lantern of pitch pine or by listening very intently to the sounds of the deer feeding. The Chief tells how he himself, in pitch darkness, shot a deer just below the ear.

Although hunting was an important and time-consuming occupation for most tribes, many were farmers as well as hunters. Some tribes were completely nomadic and followed the herds of game; others moved the entire tribe on an extended hunting trip after the crops had been harvested, while some just made short hunting trips in small bands.

Fishing

Some tribes, such as the Pueblo, considered fish taboo, but most excelled at fishing and enjoyed the peace and contemplation of angling. They used rods and lines with hooks made from shells or bone, harpoons, and seine and pursenets made of plaited vines. They caught fish in their hands by "tickling"

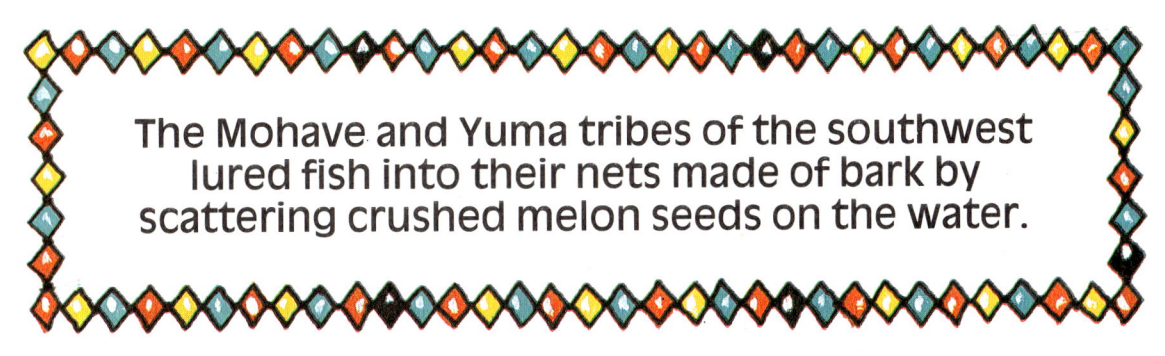

> The Mohave and Yuma tribes of the southwest lured fish into their nets made of bark by scattering crushed melon seeds on the water.

Fishing for salmon by night.

The Yahi of Northern California used two-pronged harpoons for salmon fishing. Together with the Uana, a related tribe, their estimated numbers were 3,820, but they are now extinct.

> Southeastern tribes knew of a root which would make fish unconscious without poisoning them. The Indians ground up the root and threw it into the river. Then, they only had to wait for the fish to float to the surface ready to be caught. The Pomos of Northern California used soap-root in the rivers to drug trout so that they would float to the surface.

them, and built dams and weirs to funnel the fish and make them easier to catch in pens made of reeds and osiers.

The western seaboard, from Alaska to California, was a particularly rewarding fishing ground. Salmon from the rivers was the staple food of the Tlingit, Haida, Kwakiutl, and Chinook tribes of the northwest coast, who also caught whales, sea lions, fur seals, sea otters, halibut, herring, smelt, and candlefish from the sea. They also scooped or dug up shellfish, such as lobsters, crabs, oysters, and clams.

Schools of herring came close to the shore to spawn. They were so numerous that a tool called a herring-rake, which was a pole with bone teeth set along it, could be swept through the water to spear several fish at a time. The Hupa, Karok, and Yurok tribes of California caught salmon, steelhead trout, and lampreys for food, and they prized sturgeon for making glue.

Plateau tribes built platforms over rivers, particularly near rapids, from which they could catch salmon in nets or harpoon them. Sometimes, the men dropped white stones onto the river bed beneath the platform so that the fish would show up

48

more clearly. The women were forbidden to come near the fishing sites; instead, they stayed in the camp and cleaned, skinned, and cooked the catch.

Farming

In most tribes, the women grew the crops and farmed the fields: among the Iroquois, the women owned the fields as well. An exception was found in the Pueblo villages of the Southwest, where the men worked in the fields.

By the time the first European settlers arrived, the Indians were knowledgeable, successful farmers. It

Indians catching fish with nets from canoes on the Columbia River.

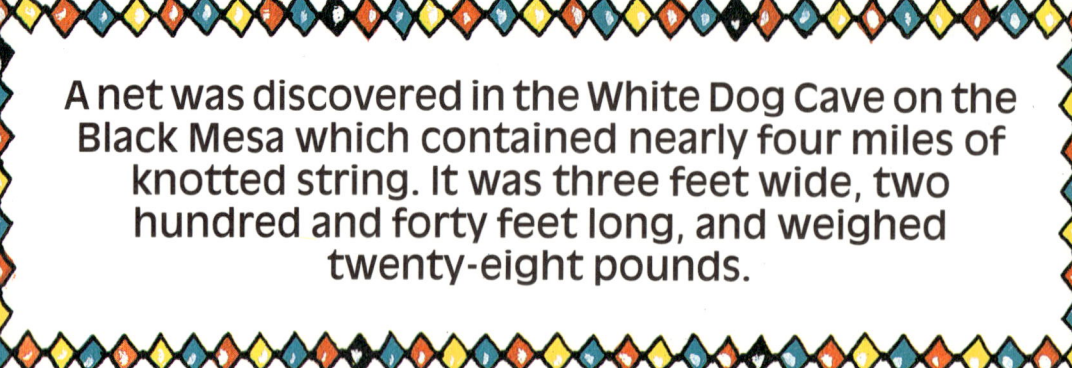

> **A net was discovered in the White Dog Cave on the Black Mesa which contained nearly four miles of knotted string. It was three feet wide, two hundred and forty feet long, and weighed twenty-eight pounds.**

was largely through their help that the newcomers got through their first year. The Indians taught the whites to grow corn, tomatoes, potatoes, and tobacco.

The Pueblo tribes also grew squash, beans, apples, peaches, and melons. The men tilled the fields, harvested the crops, and herded the flocks of sheep.

The Pimas used old irrigation canals dug by their ancestors, the Hohokam, to grow corn, kidney beans, squash, wheat, tobacco, and cotton. The Havasupai, who lived along the Colorado River, grew sunflower seeds as well as corn, squash, beans, and tobacco in fields near the base of Cataract Canyon. Among the Creeks, each family grew corn, beans, and pumpkins in its own garden plot. In addition, everyone helped to till the "town fields," which provided an abundance of food which was available

> **Two ingenious Indian methods of catching waterfowl unawares were to swim up to them underwater using a reed as a snorkel, or to float among them disguised by wearing a gourd on the head.**

The Hopi Indians had small-scale garden style plots to grow their crops.

for visitors or anyone who needed it.

The Indians did not generally herd animals until the Spanish introduced domesticated sheep and goats. The Navajo were, and still are, successful herdswomen; they use the wool for weaving their distinctive blankets as well as eating the meat. The "Civilized Tribes" of the Cherokee and Choctaw owned large herds of cattle before the tribes were forcibly removed westward to "Indian Territory" between 1831 and 1838.

Foraging

The women and children also did most of the foraging for food. Wild plants provided an important part of the diet in most tribes. In the Southwest, the Pima people collected the bean-like seed of the mesquite

51

Indians grew a wide variety of crops.

Maize

Tobacco Plant

Potatoes

Tomatoes

Squash

Apples

Peaches

Kidney Beans

Melon

tree. The Papago ate the hearts of the mescal cactus after cooking them for several days in a pit-oven to make them tender. Both tribes used wooden tongs to collect the fruits of various cacti. The giant cactus, saguaro, bears fruit which is similar to a fig, which the Pima ate fresh or dried. They also made the fruit into a syrup.

Around the Great Lakes and the headwaters of the Mississippi lived tribes such as the Menominee ("Rice People"), Ojibwa (or Chippewa), Potawatomi, Mascouten, Sauk and Fox, Miami, Illinois, Ottawa ("Traders"), Winnebago, and Eastern Dakota. Wild rice (*Zizania aquatica*), which grows plentifully in the shallow lakes and streams of the area, was an extremely useful supplement to their food supplies. It was an easy crop to harvest from a canoe. The women simply bent the stalks of the plants over the sides of the canoe and beat out the ears of grain into it.

Right: Poles from the tepee were used to make the travois.

Trade

There is evidence that tribes traded with each other from earliest times. In addition to flint weapons, copper implements and ornaments made around Lake Superior traveled as far as both coasts of the continent. The Ottawa traded pipes made from catlinite, a mineral quarried in their area.

The white settlers brought horses; guns; metal tools; weapons and utensils; cloth; liquor; and brightly colored beads and paint. After their arrival, trading became even more widespread and important. The Europeans particularly valued the fine furs trapped and cured by the Indian and some of their handicrafts, such as woolen blankets. Land, including Manhattan Island, was also bartered for goods, and slaves were traded with other tribes.

Travel and transport

In both the Northwest and the Eastern Woodlands, where there were many lakes and rivers, canoes were the usual means of travel and transport. They were made of birch-bark or were dugouts hollowed from tree trunks. Among the tribes of the Plains, the travois was used. This frame was made by lashing

> Algonquins made a horn out of birchbark. With it, they could imitate a moose call to decoy moose near enough to kill them.

together at one end two main upright poles of the tepee to make a V-shaped trolley which could be harnessed to a dog or, later, a horse. The rest of the tepee supports and the family's belongings were then loaded on and pulled to the next camp site. Horses were also used as beasts of burden.

Among the nomadic tribes, the whole population traveled around in a generally agreed area, although there were tribal wars fought over territory. Trading expeditions were usually undertaken by small groups of young men.

In various ways, most tribes lived in reasonable comfort and security without the conveniences we take for granted. They revered Mother Earth and understood that everything in the natural world is interdependent. Perhaps with our current concerns about ecological and environmental damage, we should look more closely at the ancient wisdom of the native Americans.

> Some California tribes used dentalium, a kind of shell, as money. The shells were threaded on a string and carried in purses made of antler. Hupa men had measures tattooed on their arms to check the value of a string.

Glossary

adept   skillful; good at
chattels   household possessions which can be carried away
clan   a group of related families
class system   a way of organizing society in which your position, wealth, and way of life depends upon that of your parents and their family
compatriots   people from the same country
conventions   ways of behaving which are generally agreed to be right by a particular group of people or society
decoy   to trick; ensnare; to lead into a trap
democratic   allowing everyone equal rights in making decisions about the way they are governed
descent   being descended from; taking the name of. Americans generally trace their descent through their fathers, which means that a child bears his or her father's last name
dominant   taking the lead; the one who makes decisions or acts as leader
ecological   the way in which plants, animals, and humans affect each other in the natural world
endeavors   efforts
environment   the world around us, particularly the living things
forage   to go and search for food in the fields and woods
Industrial Revolution, the   the time from the end of the eighteenth century to the beginning of the nineteenth when a great many inventions and machines were discovered. It changed the way of life for many people in Europe from farming in villages to working in factories in cities.

Glossary

initiated going through ceremonies before being allowed to join a group or society
nomadic wandering; having no fixed home
moiety a group of phratries
morals beliefs about what is right and wrong or good and evil
moss-bag a bag, lined with moss, used for carrying babies on a cradleboard
osier a species of willow
phratry a group of clans
purse nets a net shaped like a bag with cords around the opening which can be pulled tight to close the bag
role the way in which one is expected to behave
sachem a chief or leader
seine net a net used for fishing which has weights at the bottom and floats at the top. A shoal of fish can be encircled with the net and then hauled ashore
shaman medicine man; priest
spawn to produce eggs or young fish
taboo a forbidden thing
technology the application of science; using machines and electronics to solve problems and save work
tepee or tipi conical tent made of poles and buffalo hide. Used by the Plains Indians.

Table of Tribes

This list shows some of the most important Indian tribes of North America, the regions in which they lived and the languages spoken.

FAR NORTH
Algonguin; Macro-Algonkian
Beaver; Na-Dene
Beothuk; Language group unknown
Carrier; Na-Dene
Chilcotin; Na-Dene
Chipewyan; Na-Dene
Cree; Macro-Algonkian
Dogrib; Na-Dene
Hare; Na-Dene
Kaska; Na-Dene
Koyukon; Na-Dene
Kutchin; Na-Dene
Micmac; Macro-Algonkian
Montagnais; Macro-Algonkian
Naskapi; Macro-Algonkian
Ottawa; Macro-Algonkian
Sarsi; Na-Dene
Slave; Na-Dene
Tanaina; Na-Dene
Tutchone; Na-Dene
Yellowknife; Na-Dene

NORTHWEST COAST
Bella Coola; Language group unknown
Chilkat; Na-Dene
Chinook; Penutian
Coast Salish; Language group unknown
Haida; Na-Dene
Klikitat; Penutian
Kwakiutl; Language group unknown
Nootka; Language group unknown
Quileute; Language group unknown
Quinault; Language group unknown
Tlingit; Na-Dene
Tsimshian; Penutian

CALIFORNIA-INTERMOUNTAIN
Bannock; Aztec-Tanoan
Cayuse; Penutian
Chumash; Hokan
Diegueño; Hokan
Flathead; Language group unknown
Gabrielino; Aztec-Tanoan
Gosiute; Aztec-Tanoan
Hupa; Na-Dene
Interior Salish; Language group unknown
Karok; Hokan
Klamath; Penutian
Kutenai; Language group unknown
Maidu; Penutian
Modoc; Penutian
Mohave; Hokan
Nez Percé; Penutian
Paiute; Aztec-Tanoan
Pomo; Hokan
Shoshoni; Aztec-Tanoan
Ute; Aztec-Tanoan
Wintun; Penutian

SOUTHWEST
Apache; Na-Dene
Cochimi; Hokan
Havasupai; Hokan
Maricopa; Hokan
Navajo; Na-Dene
Papago; Aztec-Tanoan
Pima; Aztec-Tanoan
Pueblo:
   Acoma; Language group unknown
   Hopi; Aztec-Tanoan
   Laguna; Language group unknown
   San Ildefonso; Aztec-Tanoan
   Taos; Aztec-Tanoan
   Zia; Language group unknown
Zuñi; Language group unknown
Waiguri; Hokan
Yaqui; Aztec-Tanoan
Yuma; Hokan

PLAINS
Arapaho; Macro-Algonkian
Arikara; Macro-Siouan
Assiniboin; Macro-Siouan
Atakapa; Macro-Algonkian
Blackfeet:
   Blood; Macro-Algonkian
   Piegan; Macro-Algonkian
Caddo; Macro-Siouan
Cheyenne; Macro-Algonkian
Comanche: Aztec-Tanoan
Crow; Macro-Siouan
Gros Ventre; Macro-Algonkian
Hidatsa; Macro-Siouan

Iowa; Macro-Siouan
Kansa; Macro-Siouan
Karankawa; Language group unknown
Kiowa; Aztec-Tanoan
Mandan; Macro-Siouan
Missouri; Macro-Siouan
Omaha; Macro-Siouan
Osage; Macro-Siouan
Pawnee; Macro-Siouan
Ponca; Macro-Siouan
Quapaw; Macro-Siouan
Sioux; (Dakotah):
   Oglala; Macro-Siouan
   Santee; Macro-Siouan
   Sisseton; Macro-Siouan
   Teton; Macro-Siouan
   Yankton; Macro-Siouan
Wichita; Macro-Siouan

EASTERN WOODLANDS
Abnaki; Northeast; Macro-Algonkian
Calusa; Southeast; Macro-Siouan
Cherokee; Southeast; Macro-Siouan
Chickasaw; Southeast; Macro-Algonkian
Chippewa; Northeast & Far North; Macro-Algonkian
Chitimacha; Southeast; Macro-Algonkian
Choctaw; Southeast; Macro-Algonkian
Conestoga; Northeast; Macro-Siouan
Creek; Southeast; Macro-Algonkian
Delaware (Lenape); Northeast; Macro-Algonkian
Huron; Northeast; Macro-Siouan
Illinois; Northeast; Macro-Algonkian
Iroquois; Northeast; Macro-Siouan
Kickapoo; Northeast; Macro-Algonkian
Malecite; Northeast; Macro-Algonkian
Massachusetts; Northeast; Macro-Algonkian
Menominee; Northeast; Macro-Algonkian
Miami; Northeast; Macro-Algonkian
Missisauga; Northeast; Macro-Algonkian
Mohican; Northeast; Macro-Algonkian
Natchez; Southeast; Macro-Algonkian
Potawatomi; Northeast; Macro Algonkian
Powhatan; Southeast; Macro-Algonkian
Sauk; Northeast; Macro-Algonkian
Seminole; Southeast; Macro-Algonkian
Shawnee; Southeast; Macro-Algonkian
Timucua; Southeast; Language group unknown
Tuscarora; Southeast; Macro-Siouan
Wampanoag; Northeast; Macro-Algonkian
Winnebago; Northeast; Macro-Siouan

Tribal Areas

THE FAR NORTH AREA

Algonquin	Dogrib	Naskapi
Beaver	Hare	Ottawa
Beothuk	Kaska	Sarsi
Carrier	Koyukon	Slave
Chilcotin	Kutchin	Tanaina
Chipewyan	Micmac	Tutchone
Cree	Montagnais	Yellowknife

THE NORTHWEST COAST AREA

Chinook
Haida
Klikitat
Kwakiutl
Nootka
Quileute
Quinault
Tlingit
Tsimshian

CALIFORNIA-INTERMOUNTAIN

Bannock	Karok	Mohave
Cayuse	Klamath	Nez Percé
Chumash	Kutenai	Paiute
Flathead	Luiseno	Pomo
Gosiute	Maidu	Shoshoni
Hupa	Modoc	Ute
		Wintun

THE SOUTHWEST AREA

Apache	Laguna
Cochimi	San Ildefonso
Navajo	Taos
Papago	Zia
Pima	Zuñi
Pueblo:	Waiguri
Acoma	Yaqui
Hopi	Yuma

THE PLAINS AREA

Arapaho	Crow	Pawnee
Arikara	Gros Ventre	Ponca
Assiniboin	Hidatsa	Quapaw
Atakapa	Iowa	Sioux:
Blackfeet:	Kansa	Oglala
Blood	Karankawa	Santee
Plegan	Kiowa	Sisseton
Caddo	Mandan	Teton
Cheyenne	Omaha	Yankton
Comanche	Osaga	Wichita

THE EASTERN WOODLANDS AREA

NORTHEAST
Abnaki
Chippewa
Delaware
Erie
Fox
Huron
Illinois
Iroquois:
  Cayuga
  Mohawk
  Onondaga
  Oneida
  Seneca
Kickapoo
Mahican
Malecite

Massachusetts
Menominee
Miami
Mohegan
Narraganset
Potawatomi
Sauk
Susquehanna
Wampanoag
Winnebago

SOUTHEAST
Calusa
Cherokee
Chickasaw

Chitimacha
Choctaw
Creek
Natchez
Powhatan
Seminole
Shawnee
Timucua
Tuscarora
Yamasee
Yuchi

The major linguistic areas

Key
- Eskimo Aleut
- Algonkian
- Aztec-Tanoan
- Iroquian
- Other Groups
- Na-Dene
- Macro-Siouan

Index

Numbers in *italics* refer to illustrations.

Alaska 48
angling 45
animals 38-40, 50, 51, 56
armor 11, 34

babies 21-23
bands 6, 11, 45
Bear Lake 11
bears 38, 39
Black Elk 15
Black Mesa 50
blow guns 34
boats 10, 55
bolas 40
bows and arrows 32-3, 38, 39, *39*
British Columbia 8, 11, 23, 24, 33, 34
buffalo 38, 39, 41, *7, 31, 42-3*

cactus 54
California 47, 48, 56
canoe 8, 10, 18, *49, 52-3*, 54, 55
captives 31
Cataract Canyon 50
Catlin, George *7*
catlinite 54
charms 21
chiefs 9-11, 17, 25
children 7, 15, 17-23, 51
Civilized Tribes, the 51
clans 6-8, 12, 17, 38, 57
clubs (societies) 12
clubs (weapons) 34
Colorado River 50
Columbia River *49*
copper 54
corn 50
council 11-12

coup 26, 27, *31*
cradleboards 21-3, *21, 22*
crime and punishment 11
crops 50

dams 48
dancing 12
deer 39, *39*, 44-5
dentalium 56
divorce 16
dogs 41
dream 26, 37

eagles 7-8
Eastern Woodlands 21, 31, 34, 55
education 18-9
Europeans 6, 31, 49, 54
elections 12
family 6-8
farming 45, 49-51
fishing 17, 45-9, *49*
flint 54
foraging 17, 18, 51-4
fruit 17
fur 54

gambling 24
game 6, 39
games 23-4
Glacier National Park *25*
glue 48
Grand Medicine Society 12
Great Basin 41
Great Lakes, the 54
guardian spirit 7
guns 37-8, 44, 54

harpoons 8, 32, 45, 47, 48
healing 12
herring 48
High Horse 16
horses 16, 25, 28, 32, 38, 54
hunting 17, 29, 38-45, *39, 41, 42-3*, 56
husbands 16

Indian Territory 51
irrigation 50
Iroquois, The League of the 11-12
Kah-ge-ga-gah-bowh, Chief 44-5
Kishkekosh *31*
knives 34-45

Lake Superior 54
Louisiana 40

machinery 6
magic 37
marriage 7, 8, 12, 15-6, *15*
medicine man 12, 15
mescal 54
mesquite 51-4
Mississippi, the 54
moieties 8
money 58
Montana *25*
moss bags 21, *21*, 56

Neihardt, John G. 15
nets 41, *49*, 50
Newfoundland 38
nomads 45, 56, 58
Northwest Canada 34
Northwest Plateau 23
Northwest Territories 23

ordeals 18

Pacific coast 18
phratries 8, 58
pipes 54
pits 41
Plains Indians 16, 18, 27, 37, 38, 55

63

Plateau tribes 48
poison 33, 34
pottery 18
prisoners 31
punishment 11

relatives 7
religion 12
rivers 10, 48, 55
Rocky Mountains 38, 40

sachem 9-11, 58
salmon 47, 48
scalping 26, 27, 31
school 18
settlers 6, 54
sewing 17
shaman 12-58
shell 22, 56

shellfish 48
shield 34-7
Short Bull 34
slaves 31, 54
snares 41, 44
societies 12
Southwest, the 45, 49, 51
Spanish 32, 38, 51
spear 32, 45
steel 34
stone 32, 33
sunflowers 50

tattoo 18
tepee 7, 18, 25, 54
Texas 7
tobacco 38, 50
tomahawk 34
torture 31, 31

totem 7
trade 6, 10, 34, 37-8, 54, 56
travois 54, 55-6
tribe 8, 9, 12, 17, 38, 45

Ursus Ferox 38

vision 26

war 11, 12, 18, 25-9, 38, 56
weapons 18, 32-38, 54
weaving 18, 51
weirs 48
whales 8, 48
wheel 6
White Dog Cave 50
wild rice 52-3, 54
wives 11, 16
women 12, 17, 18, 23, 26, 49, 51, 54

Index of tribes

Numbers in *italics* refer to illustrations.

Algonquin 21, 31, 56
Apache 22, 29, 31, 37
Beothuk 38
Blackfeet 25
Carrier 11
Cayuga 12
Cherokee 34, 51
Chinook 48
Chippewa 54
Choctaw 34, 51
Comanche 7, 26, 29, 31
Creek 50
Crow 16
Eastern Dakota 54
Flathead 23
Fox 31, 54
Haida 8, 18, 48
Havasupai 50

Hohokam 50
Hupa 48, 56
Illinois 54
Interior Salish 33
Iroquois 11-12, 17, 18, 34, 49
Karok 48
Kutenai 23
Kutchin 23
Kwakiutl 48
Mascouten 54
Menominee 54
Miami 54
Micmac 38
Mohawk 11
Mohave 45
Natchez 8
Navajo 16, 51
Nez Perce 21
Nootka 8
Oglala Sioux 15

Ojibwa 10, 12, 44-5, 54
Omaha 12
Oneida 12
Onondaga 12
Ottawa 54
Papago 54
Pima 50, 51, 52
Pomo 40, 48
Potawatomi 54
Pueblo 8, 45, 49, 50
Salish 23
Sauk 54
Seneca 12
Sioux 34
Slave 34
Tlingit 48
Tuscarora 12
Yahi 47
Yana 47
Yuma 45
Yurok 48